DEDICATION

This book is dedicated to Her Excellency Dr. Ngozi OkonjoIweala (The Director General World Trade Organization) For her resilience struggles in educating women on how to: experience life outside of comfort zone to get good judgement that can be used in solving problem; judiciously engage in actions that will lead to becoming a person of substance; identify with the sentiment that "If you are not part of the solution, then you are part of the problem"; nurture the early behaviour of a girl child and get her mind-set competitively ready to be able to bridge the awkward gap created by boys learning to compete while girls learn to get along; and to take cognizance of the fact that Good problem solving between competing interests typically requires a person of sound judgement who has immense empathy, complete objectivity and solid life-honed values etc.

ACKNOWLEDGEMENT

My special thanks go to God Almighty who amidst my follies and frailties as a man shows infinite mercies on me. Whatever credit or commendation there is for the publication of this work, I share it with my amiable wife, Mrs Precious Arista Mejeh and my 3 kids Peniel, Jason and Zinnia.

PREFACE

'Behind a Woman of Substance' is coined after a holistic assessment of a 'lifestyle'. Is a book that really wants to show women a way out, to walk up to the same line as men but not get painted with a stereotypical paintbrush. To empower women to take proper credit for their actions because they erroneously hide their success under shadows. It straightens the way forward and embraces the abundant synergy of man and the woman to sublimate and make an arduous task less herculean.

This book also emphasises the right way to nurture the early behaviour of a girl child and get her mindset competitively ready to be able to bridge the awkward gap created by boys learning to compete while girls learn to get along. It brings to light the barrier of self-doubt that women frequently create, and shows why it is critical that women step up to the plate and fall into their natural roles as world leaders. It clears these bugs and design flaws of the mind and provides active choices among many plausible alternatives.

As a potential superpower, the images created here will nullify the stereotypes that plague women in scenes of competitions and workplaces and will judiciously reconstruct and shape her day to day activities that will bring out strong leadership skills that rival those same skills in a man. The traits women have are a natural fit for a leadership model that promotes empathy and consensus-building. So it gives women even more ammunition to break down the long-protected image of men running the operations as women claw their way to the middle.

Indeed 'Behind a Woman of Substance' is a masterpiece. Readers will find the book a valuable source of information for application to help restore the dignity of a woman and extricate them from the impending opprobrium.

CHAPATER ONE

TAKING THE NECESSARY RISK

It is very delicate issue in general when a man speaks about the role of a woman, because many opinions about this are very subjective, emotional and sometimes full of prejudices. There is a phenomenon in our daily life. The question was what should be done? Before a solution to this bizarre conundrum surfaced to extricate women from the impending opprobrium, and we agreed that the single most important thing about leadership is the ability to take necessary risks and contrary to gender stereotypes. Women are incredibly risk-adept; this perception doesn't always serve either sex well. But, women are different. They think differently and they "move" through society differently. Acceptance of the inherent diversity is a good thing.

I believe that risk is necessary for transformative change. People operate from a set of home behaviours because those behaviours have been successful for them most of the time. The happy thing is that human beings are intelligent, and can learn to adopt different behaviours for different situations to obtain the outcome they strive for. With practice, those other behaviours breed in us greater flexibility, resulting in better leadership. Adopting other behaviours feel risky whether man or woman. And then there's the nature and nurture thing.

Risk-taking is central to everything worthwhile. There is no single risk that will solve all your problems. To be afraid of taking a risk is not novel because the moment of committing to acting on the risk will be the most fearful part. Most of the time, you will lose something merely by deciding to risk-usually your comfort zone. Some form of separation anxiety is present in every act of risk taking. At some point you will never have enough information, so you have to act, considering your goal because a risk without a purpose is in trouble from the start. Asking questions could be the best option. "It is better to appear stupid than to make big mistakes because you are afraid of looking stupid."

The loss involved is to be taken into cognizance. If you don't expect the loss, you don't understand the risk. Women must take their risk because no one else can take your interest to heart the way you can. Recognising the need to risk and deciding to take it by asking the necessary questions: Is the potential loss greater than the gain? Who should know about this risk and why? Initiating the risk and reaching a point of no return involves commitment, self-imposed questions and answers originating from the mind. Am I trying to prove something about myself? Who are the key people involved in this risk? Do I trust their judgment? How do I know when to change plan or stop? At the end you analyse your success or failure.

In 'politics' for example, I have meticulously unravelled mysteries behind success in women politics and urges you to hog the spotlight and take your credit. Who should be a politician? "If you are honest and stand for the interest of your electors, without being selfish, but ready to make sacrifices. If you are really honest and want to change something in a way that is respectful and tolerant to other opinions, then you should become a politician – it doesn't matter if you are a man or a woman. I know that this sounds very ideal, but this is what real politicians should aspire to." "It would surely be wrong, to exclude women from politics, but it would be also wrong, to include them compulsively. It's no secret, that man and woman are different to each other. Probably that is the reason for this gender issue. They think differently, speak differently and because of that they act differently. Margaret Thatcher, an English politician once said: "If you want something to be said in politics, then refer to a man and if you want something to be done in politics, then refer to a woman." This statement is a moot point, but it illustrates, that men and women complement one another, when they join forces with each other. So we should stop thinking about gender issues if it's a question of politics and we should start looking at the person's character or behaviour. This should be the basis of good evaluations.

Women achievers are no stranger to the harsh realities of life and its impediment. They view things from a different perspective. Outstanding women politicians have answered so many puzzles in women politics to remain answered. Quite obvious the political terrain is still murky for African women because operators have decided to play it dirty, but it is obvious that some prudent and persistent women in the corridors of power are very strong advocates for more women participation in politics, especially in the parliament, where they avowed that there should be a balance both at the executive level and the legislative level. "It is a necessity and it has become imperative, at this point in time, for us to have more women in the decision making process. Until and when we do that, we will continue to perambulate in one place in Nigeria. I want Nigeria to move to the next level. There is a paradigm shift all over the world now. Women are taking over, not that we want to chase the men out; I just want us to sit down side by side and take Nigeria to the Promised Land. So I am hoping that in the next general election, Nigeria will have more women both in the Senate and in the House of Representatives." She affirmed.

It had been asserted with certainty that a woman of substance with infinite patience and planning had contributed immensely in giving solutions to the problems facing up-coming women leaders and these solutions ranges from: taking necessary risk as a woman; taking proper credit for your action; your innate power to subdue a man; deference in attitude that keep you moving; grooming a girl child to lead; self-help; learn by doing; identifying challenges of being a boss; keys to leadership; the making of a woman of **substance etc.** So do the needful, absorb them and help in flushing those areas of mediocrity in your life.

Contexts in which significant investments of time and money are placed in projects which require learning-by-doing, and where the likelihood of success is very hard to predict, we found women of substance engaged in a lot of risk-taking actions. But realistically, women and men have different views about taking risks; women often dislike going outside their comfort zone more than men do. For many women executives, it's an innate skill—but still is one, they had to nurture and cultivate throughout their careers. Others more junior often need coaching and mentoring. Women sometimes take their time figuring the lay of the land, and don't appear confident. Mentors sometimes have to push women to their next job because they get good at something and want to stay with it.

You have to take risks and have failures in your career, and stick with it. Junior ones should emulate the leaders they admire most in their organization. Born leaders embrace risk because they first embrace challenges (and risk comes with it). It's a natural leadership skill that you can also learn. It is advisable to hire and surround yourself with people who are smarter than you. Then, put them in an environment where they will succeed. That makes other sharp people want to join you. Women are always dinning with largest numerical strength, undermining its problem. Don't let the lack of headcount hold you back. You don't need to create a big kingdom; you can create a virtual army instead.

Who makes the first move has always been a problem in women's folk. Be open to different kinds of experiences. For example, consider taking an assignment that no one else wants. Don't be afraid of blending your technical and business acumen. Having a technology cornerstone is crucial; women shouldn't be afraid to take assignments that surface, as long as you have this cornerstone. Don't fear being viewed as technical-the business world is fast becoming technology pervasive. Don't be afraid to speak up because someone may judge you. If you are completely honest and transparent, you can come out well in the end. Leaders need the courage to say, "It's not working," which might mean putting yourself out of a job. Do it anyway. Taking risk must first be viewed in the light of your passion over it. It is vital to overlook an assignment if you are not passionate over it. Nothing is worth doing if you're not excited about it. If you're excited, you are more willing to walk the plank a little more.

What is your mind-set towards risk? Necessary risk has to be taken. Make sure you are on solid ground, especially when launching into something new and risky. Sell your idea to others and link it to business outcomes. Often, success is about how you find other experts. Ways to drive revenue in new business ideas. There's a lot more oversight, many new business ideas are hard to connect to revenue so you have to work it out. Understand how the economy downturn impacts risk taking. Life in the business-world is not a "roller coaster ride". Things could go wrong. Don't shut the door of analysis by paralysis because you want to cover things that could go wrong. This kind of thinking restricts creativity and innovation. If you have a natural inhibition to risks, work to overcome it. Think positive, see a plan, and change your perspective to focus on the benefits. Eventually risk can catch up with most people and hurts their reputation if it is illegal or immoral.

It is very important to know that everyone has a personal brand, it might not be visible. But you have to recognise that fact, even if you are unaware of it. Everything you do contributes to your personal branding, so it is important to consciously know it is and then shape it. Sex play important role in this act of branding because your way is different from the way of a man because stereotypes are strongly held. Rather, facilitate meetings by initiating ideas and asking questions that subtly draw points and allowing team of peers to accept your suggestions. Women need to walk up to the same line as men but not get painted with a stereotypical paintbrush.

CHAPTER TWO
TAKING PROPER CREDIT FOR YOUR ACTION

Everything in life is first judged by its appearance, you cannot assess what is unseen and it counts for nothing. "Never let you get lost in the crowd or buried in oblivion." Is a wise saying, Stand out; be conspicuous by properly communicating what you have achieved and even allying with known risk-takers within an organisation. Communicating your achievements allow you to generate good publicity and keep your profile high. Set your partnership achievable targets and shout about it when you achieve them. Don't be shy. Success attracts support and that support can help partnership to flourish.

Women erroneously hide their success under shadows. Just like a man needs his wife, the woman needs her husband too, as both synergies the way forward and sublimate to make the arduous task less herculean. People with good public relation skills are not to be left out in this trend. Some people are naturally sociable and have a way of assuaging hardliners. So, including such personalities on your steering group can be a good way to help ensure that your successes are widely communicated. "Press friendly" cannot be overemphasized, just be sure to get them to sign a confidentiality agreement first so they only share the information that you are ready to release.

In the spirit of being welcoming to all, women managers need to remember that an adult's experience of the high rank is not the only one that is important. Kids are the decision makers of the future and entertaining them will do wonders in your quest to actualize you dream because they play important role in keeping your name on their lips and continue to fan the flame of intimacy in the type of relationship a woman will keep while in power. There are plenty of imaginative events and activities which could be hosted to keep children occupied, particularly during breaks. Sometimes local groups will want to provide something but don't have the resources on their own - so get them together and see what you might be able to offer collectively.

Team members are to be handled with care no matter their status, acknowledging their efforts will go a long way to smooth your track because if you handle them with respect, you will see them sticking out their necks for you. Yes this might be uncomfortable, but an assertive. Straight forward discussion shows that you are watching their effort. The credit look is very deceitful; don't be greedy to share it if you don't want others to take it. Don't be afraid of spotlight, share it when the going gets good and also take your blame when you make mistake. That action of yours will go a long way to influence others. Demonstrate the same respect you want to receive.

The fact that team work is very important in politics, does not call for ransacking; it has to be prevented arbinitio. Being team spirited and concentrating deeply to find solution to challenging problems is an attribute; this doesn't mean that one will always create a vacuum for unwarranted leakage because your strategy must be accorded the necessary security for others not to take credit for what are rightfully in your ideas. The axiom is doing the job you need to do and getting credit for it. If you are working hard and coming up with ideas that have the potential benefit to your establishment, you need to protect them.

Colleagues hijack ideas easily and out-manoeuvre the inventor. This is a case that affect adversely on women because of their simple mien. A climbing game does create an avenue for bold approach, everyone will likely appreciate the extra effort you put into a plan. But you have to prevent it from being hijacked. So the best way to do that is to develop an implementation idea and present it as an addendum, though it might form the real thing but hold on to it till the right and appropriate time to take your credit. Office politics could not be left out of this. When submitting your idea to your immediate superior, do extra search and hold it to yourself. At that time some would try to be more subtle and present the idea without given you the desired credit, and then at this juncture, your extra data that was not in the original would make you the expert without any contrary opinion from your superior. Granted, politicians and other executives love to extol the virtues of a team mentality; all claiming that team work is pretty much the solution to everything. The smart way to avoid being used is to let the lesser ideas belong to the team or the people; this will still earn you the reputation of being a team player. Mind you, you are not always going to get the credit of your team playing. Do less talking and communicate through actions. For example, People's belief about women in politics need to be shaken and proven wrong. Nigerians' knowledge of this game need to be updated by opening a floor to know why there are doubts. Try to clean up their opposing belief with answers which you have compiled by using your imagination to envision the possibility. This is exactly why women work so hard to distinguish themselves from the rest of men, let's be honest. It's those special projects and great presentations that make Dr. Ngozi Okonjo-Iweala valuable member of a team.

Real women are so diplomatic, so adroit at handling people. Yes because they believe the simple truth of speaking all the good they know about that person. It is not good to criticize, condemn and complain. Dealing with people is not dealing with creature of logic to the best of my knowledge, but dealing with creature of emotion, creatures bristling with prejudices and motivated by pride and vanity. You want to get them? Then make them to do it! Criticism is a crude method with sharply undesirable repercussions. Dr Dewey said that the deepest urge in human nature is "the desire to be important." Everybody likes a compliment. It is very gnawing and unfaltering human hunger, and it is very rare to get people who will stoop to satisfy this heart hunger, when you do, you will definitely hold people in the palm.

It is this desire for a feeling of importance that inspired Nelson Mandela to write his "Long Walk to Freedom." This desire inspired this woman of substance to rise from her somnolent zone to the field of world politics and set unprecedented pace in the history of democratic experiment: that it is possible for a woman to rise from its slumbering state and get totally integrated into men's dominated society. This desire would make you to go for the latest car, wear the latest material and talk about your brilliant performances. It is this desire that lures many into dangerous lives. Sometimes people became invalid just to win sympathy and attention so as to become important. This is not strange to women judging from their life in pregnancy and the hysteria accompanying it. There is nothing more than appreciation and encouragement. There is nothing that kills ambitions of a person than to criticise, be anxious to praise and loathe to find fault.

Creating good human relationship, live 70% (seventy per cent) of your wide spread publicity to the unknown. This might sound outlandish to you. It is an important common canon sense. The way you represent people's opinion creates indelible imprint in their ability to carry you to unknown destination where you least expected to reach. "If there is any one secret of success," said Henry Ford, "it lies in the ability to get the other person's point of view and see things from the person's angle as well as from your own."

This is an open truth but majority ignore it. If after reading this book you absorb powers bestowed in an upgraded tendency to think always in terms of other people's views, and see things from their angle- if you get that key thing out of this book, it may easily prove to be one of the building blocks of your career, politically or otherwise. Looking at other people's point of view and arousing in them an eager want for something is not to be construed as manipulating the person so that he/she will do something that is only for your benefit and his/her detriment. Each party should gain from the negotiation.

Don't be afraid to show emotions because is a vital part of communication. The fact that we have different dispositions does not blur keen observation from identifying the truth behind ones mood and tone. When it is time to sober over a misdeed, shade controllable tears but do not cut your communication because that will be the appropriate time to pass the message across. At that time, impart the way forward to solve and manage the problem. You are being part of their lives in one way or the other. And there is not necessarily a solution for every problem; however, every problem can be managed positively. Your potential achievement would go a long way to wipe the tears you shaded before the congregation. Sure there is a problem which you are promising to put in a proper perspective. It is a hard-core principle and not a vague attitude.

CHAPTER THREE
THE POWER TO SUBDUE

A man's self-esteem can be given easy access when he is subdued. In building a moralistic standard that will influence your man, first acknowledge the big picture and positive qualities of his. Unravelling the mystery surrounding your influence over a man, a woman should understand how literally a man takes words, what his intimacy is really about, his intent or purpose etc. The axiom is love. Love brings out the zeal to acknowledge all these qualities in your man and help to place them at the appropriate positions. Using your soft voice to melt hard objects and assert authority in your man cannot be overemphasized. A woman will use these qualities to her advantage to point out her way forward and be free from shackles of domestic servitude because you have captured and impaired the decision making part of the man.

Whether in politics, homes or offices, Men are weak and could easily succumb to women's manipulations. It is their destiny to be controlled by women and they should understand that they have more influence over their men than they think because a man will try to live up to the image his wife has for him. The language of men are hopes and dreams, when a woman shares her dream for a conquest that will help in actualizing her man's dream, the man submits and obey her. Words should be used cautiously as not to sting self-esteem and you see a man launching into defence by interpreting meaning of words and you wonder why he is hearing them in more sweeping terms. Use words that are not concretely definable on your man in faulting him and get going without creating a scene.

Getting attention through action involves marrying out of potentials and not who he is, because you believe you could improve his status when you settle down with him. Your man can still downgrade your effort to improve him, as a slack to his self-esteem. Still make him look enraptured and always complement first before criticizing constructively. First acknowledge the big picture - "I know you're an intelligent gentleman who would be unwilling to take nonsense, I'm still wondering why you stoop too low to be this insignificant" - the criticism doesn't sting.   It does not mean a woman should spend the rest of her life in patronage. But acknowledging your man's complete picture improves your power to subdue and walk through.

Men have penchant for sense of significance when you impact it in them. A man will feel more motivated to please a woman if he feels you think the world of him. At this acceleration point, a man will allow a woman to rise and Move Mountains with his name just to live up to the image of responsible and caring you have posited of him. The fact about these skills is the checks and balances which you have given to his "Ego and feelings" to outline the distinction between them and their workability which shows emotional identity and protect his sense of significance because they differ in intensity and consequences.

Ego can still be damaged mistakenly and you see who's usually quick to forgive arguments with females, completely refused to forget yours, and things continue to be very weird and awkward between you. You didn't understand why that was, and you have already apologized but at the same time, you don't want to overly try to appease him in case you lose his respect. Solution is to find ways to admire him, tell him about it, and do it gently, patiently, smilingly, and in bits and pieces. You will find magical resolution. It has been proved by psychoanalysts that "male's ego" has automatic negative connotation so avoid ego stroking.

Some men can be easily offended and grudge-holding or vindictive, but is not a red flag. Some might say it's a red flag signifying that he has a high degree of self-loathing or self-hatred. This is where you have to assess if his sense of significance has been 'damaged', because his sense of self admiration hinges on what and how you think of him more than on manly accomplishments because his internalizing about his present life keeps him focused away from future accomplishments. He might have been probably jerked up and now he probably can't grow up. When you hurt a man's pride, he can get pretty nasty.

A woman has to tap into her feminine power to inspire her man's love and affection. Men treat women with the respect they deserve. If you've been used to settling for less in a relationship, stop right now. Don't put up with poor treatment from a man; don't think you don't deserve a better treatment from a man. Learn to love yourself by embracing all of yourself, even the parts you don't like. When you look your best, you will begin to feel your best and you will become more sensitive to yourself instead of always being sensitive to him. As you stay busy doing the things you love and pursuing your interest, you will grow to a likable personality with powers to dictate your pace in field of endeavour.

CHAPTER FOUR
DEFERENCE IN ATTITUDE

It is time for women to start attacking the problem and not the person responsible for the problem. Actually, this might sound outlandish to you but it is time to impact yourself with the sports-modelled, competitive culture of men. Men focus on money and status, and learn to work according to its rules. The unassailable truth is that in working assiduously to adhere to this rule, the inner selves have to be intact, betraying it can endanger zeal to forge ahead courageously. Winning matters a lot in men's sports world. The early behaviour and mind-set of a girl has to be nurtured competitively to be able to bridge the awkward gap created by boys learning to compete while girls learn to get along.

Every relationship needs a balance of give and take; it is abnormal and awkward attempt to devalue yourself when you think of how you will please him by actively engaging in something to show him why he should be attracted to you and interested in you. These efforts are not what will make a man move for actual steps but the attitudes in you. Its cornerstone is a healthy sense of self-esteem. Because you know your wants and your boundaries, you would be able to ascertain dangerous move to cross it and give a warning that shows the unacceptability. The hands can't be properly washed if the both did not engage in the exercise.

A woman needs a man that will give her what she needs emotionally and what a woman wants in love life has to be determined by her attitude. Men can be attracted by this at a deep level and get inspired or turn around if they are not ready to give what you want. What you want does not stop a man from his goals and dreams, relationship can only be passionate and interesting when both nourish their particular passion.

Taking responsibility for your happiness shows a strong sense of a woman who knows what she needs. It is an irresistible attitude that can attract a man and also position and score you high in man's order of priority. A woman should know what to do to get there without engaging in a game play to convince a man. Your attitude should be modelled in such a way that shows your ability to take a decision and stand by it without being intimidated by the opposite sex.

Nonverbal communication skills in a woman should not be weak at all, to allow her a space in taking a stand boldly, eye contact and movement can say a lot about a person's attitude and personality, it has to be used to tackle the bad times in a matured way. In most part of the world, keeping one's gaze down is considered as a sign of low confidence, poor self-esteem and weak personality. Furthermore, looking away from person while speaking is a sign of disinterest and dishonest. Arrogance and rebellion can also be attributed to a habit of making eye contact and movement a lot while speaking. It is also a very efficient way of expressing ones emotion. It's true that eye is the window to one's soul; it's easy to guess if someone is lying, sorry, happy, suspicious, hurt or uncomfortable etc. by looking into his or her eyes.

Your habitual walk speaks volumes; always walk in with a good posture to match. Be intentional as you stop to chat or engage others so that you don't communicate a lack of confidence. There are several concepts invoking the appearance of the permanent characteristic of an individual, so know what you communicate when you walk. Current state of a person's emotions and attitudes should be analysed with posture in the context of other messages both verbal and nonverbal.

Successful woman's nonverbal communication skills can be found in Robert Phipps' analysis: "Head position is a great one to play around with. When you want to feel confident and self-assured keep your head level both horizontally and vertically. You can also use this straight head position when you want to be authoritative and want what you're saying to be taken seriously. Conversely, when you want to be friendly and in the listening, receptive mode, tilt your head just a little to one side or other. You can shift the tilt from left to right at different points in the conversation.

Arms give away the clues as to how open and receptive we are to everyone we meet and interact with, so keep your arms out to the side of your body or behind your back. This shows you are not scared to take on whatever comes your way and you meet things "full frontal". In general terms the more outgoing you are as a person, the more you tend to use your arms with big movements. The quieter you are the less you move your arms away from your body. So, try to strike a natural balance and keep your arm movements' midway, when you want to come across in the best possible light, crossing the arms is a no-no in front of others. Obviously if someone says something that gets your goat, then by all means show your disapproval by crossing them!

Legs are the furthest point away from the brain, and consequently they're the hardest bits of our bodies to consciously control. They tend to move around a lot more than normal when we are nervous, stressed or being deceptive. So best to keep them as still as possible, in most situations especially at interviews or work meetings, try to be careful too in the way you cross your legs. Do you cross at the knees, ankles or bring your leg up to rest on the knee of the other? This is more a question of comfort than anything else. Just be aware that the last position mentioned is known as the "Figure Four" and is generally perceived as the most defensive leg cross, especially if it happens as someone tells you something that might be of a slightly dubious nature, or moments after (as always, look for a sequence).

Angle of the body in relation to others gives an indication of our attitudes and feelings towards them. We angle toward people we find attractive, friendly and interesting and angle ourselves away from those we don't - it's that simple! Angles include leaning in or away from people, as we often just tilt from the pelvis and lean sideways to someone to share a bit of conversation. For example, we are not in complete control of our angle neither at the cinema because of the seating nor at a concert when we stand shoulder to shoulder and are packed in like sardines. In these situations we tend to lean over towards the other person.

Hand gestures are so numerous. It's hard to give a brief guide...but here it goes. Palms slightly up and outward is seen as open and friendly. Palm down gestures are generally seen as dominant and possibly aggressive, especially when there is no movement or bending between the wrist and the forearm. This palm up, palm down is very important when it comes to handshaking and, where appropriate, we suggest you always offer a handshake upright and vertical, which should convey equality.

Distance from others is crucial if you want to give off the right signals. Stand too close and you'll be marked as "pushy" or "in your face". Stand or sit too far away and you'll be "keeping your distance" or "stand offish". Neither is what we want, so observe if in a group situation how close all the other people are to each other. Also notice if you move closer to someone and they back away - you're probably just a tiny bit too much in their personal space, their comfort zone. "You've overstepped the mark" and should pull back a little. Yes your ears play a vital role in communication with others, even though in general terms most people can't move them much, if at all. However, you've got two ears and only one mouth, so try to use them in that order. If you listen twice as much as you talk you come across as a good communicator who knows how to strike up a balanced conversation without being me, me, me or the wallflower.

Mouth movements can give away all sorts of clues. We pursue our lips and sometimes twist them to the side when we're thinking. Another occasion we might use this movement is to hold back an angry comment we don't wish to reveal. Nevertheless, it will probably be spotted by other people and although they may not comment, they will get a feeling you were not too pleased. There are also different types of smiles and each gives off a corresponding feeling to its recipient. Just changing your body language very slightly can have an amazing impact on the people around you." With proofs, all these from Phipps' analysis contribute immensely and are evident in her quest to achieving her set goals as a woman of substance.

CHAPTER FIVE
IN TIME OF ACTION

Actually, getting proper approval before acting or taking a bold step cannot be taken for granted in a world of unequal opportunities. To get ahead in life, in career, in everything, women need to stop acting like little girls and learn how to apply the rubric. A saying has it that "it is easier to get forgiveness than to get approval or permission." Children, not adults, ask for permission to do perfectly rational things.

Originality is the most beautiful aspect of life. Every individual has his or her own identity and it is the best attitude to be your real self always. When you stick to your own self, the confidence is assured. Your innate characters should be refined and practiced; the problem is not who you are, but who you think you are not. To stop acting and develop your self-confidence, you should first believe that you are the biggest asset that needs to be tapped.

It is wrong to be superficial because it will impel your real self and subjugate you to some issues that can't be interpreted. Distinguished woman and a role model (Dr. Ngozi Okonjo-Iweala) has tried to put things forward to shine some light on the horizon for women to juxtapose and experience real love in action, not "thought" of being in love, and then once something goes wrong, they find themselves in the emptiness of the relationship. She stressed out that relationship with "whatever" aren't easy; they do have problems and take lots of compromise to be able to bring back the initial fun of it. The hard to get game of a woman exposes her to words she wants to hear which might not be her true self, so in trying to live up to the meaning of those words attributed to her character, she starts dealing with the underlying issue of poor self-esteem. Try to be your real self before taking action.

It is not wrong to expect too much in life because "is absolute unreasonable to settle for less" according to John Mason. But don't be too difficult and complicated, don't look for everything because it is practically impossible to have the whole world, don't wake up in the morning and expect something to happen, wakes up and make something happen. Having a more pragmatic approach to life endears you into a real woman not a little girl no matter your age; it gives you the ability to make a heroic sacrifice, service, unselfishness and exhibit resilience in excelling to the echelon where you never expected. So act accurately if you are passion filled. People in general should realise that nobody is perfect, we all have flaws and mistakes (though there's a fine line between 'flaw' and 'ignorance'), so don't be so quick to judge but accept mistakes and give way for corrections.

From start to finish, life is nothing but a game, to be a "leader" winning must be in your lexicon. As a potential leader, you should not be part of a decision that assist in derailing 'right' by making what is right appear bad, in a bid to protect personal interest. Those act work against future, it can be done ignorantly though, but when you are awake with realities, go on your knees and ask for forgiveness and repent totally from it. The quest for a woman of substance keeps revealing secrets, unfolding events that will put your faith in jeopardy, but don't sacrifice good judgment on the altar of power obsession.

The much talk about is how to 'be a man' not how to 'be a woman', it is okay for a woman to act like a man, but a total flaw for a man to act like a woman. It is a mere interpretation; it is neither here nor there. Thus patriarchal society based on a view that subjugated nature to the spirit of man, also subjugated woman. Once we understand the historical connections between women and nature and their subsequent oppression, we cannot help but take a stand on the war against nature.

Ecofeminism gives women and men common ground. While women may have been associated with nature, this does not mean that somehow they have been socialised in a different world from men. Women have learned to think in the same dualities as men, and they feel just as alienated as do their brothers. The social system isn't good for either - or both. Yet, both are the social system. They need some common ground from which to be critically self-conscious, to enable them to recognise and affect the deep structure of their relations, with each other and with our environment. In addition to participating in forms of resistance, such as non-violent civil disobedience, women can also encourage, support and develop within our communities a cultural life which celebrates the many differences in nature, and which encourage reflection on the consequences of our actions, in all our relations. Women's values, centred on life-giving, must be re-valued, and elevated from their once-subordinate role. What women know from experience needs recognition and respect. They have had generations of experience in conciliation, dealing with interpersonal conflicts daily in domestic life. They know how to feel for others because they have been socialised that way. So to save the damning world, the dignity of a woman has to be restored.

It's very absurd to treat the world like a joke and scamper when things go wrong, real woman has to be practical and take challenges. Attach values, morals and common sense in a relationship and care less for looks because they fade the more you get to know him. Attraction is important actually, but not where you are seeking a model, that's a pretty lousy long-term investment for the sake of short-term gain, invariably, you have prostituted yourself for the sake of outward gain, and you will lose all sense of self-dignity and worth when you realise what you have done. Try to be simple in life, uncomplicated and have a good heart. You will definitely achieve your set goals.

If you pursue fowl with anger, you fall epileptically, the truth is constant and it is immaterial from any mouth it comes. In her bid to consolidate their power to take necessary action independently, a distinguished woman in one of her epochal and thought provoking speeches condemns negative cynicism among women. "Do you assume the best or the worst? Are you filled with hope or are you filled with doubt? Do you think kindly of the people around you or do you judge their motivations? At times it seems as if the whole world is absorbed in negative cynicism."

Before you can deal with anything in life you need to know a little bit about it. For example, if you want to know how to lose weight you need to learn what fat is, how you come to gain it, and then methods for getting rid of it. The same is true of negative emotions and mental states. You need to learn what it is, where it comes from and then take necessary steps to defeat it.

The Oxford English Dictionary defines cynicism in a very enlightening way: "...a disposition to disbelieve in the sincerity or goodness of human motives and action..." The main thing to notice about the definition is the presence of negativity. A cynical person will almost always choose to doubt, disbelieve or discredit, even when there is no logical reason to do so. There are many schools of thought on the matter – some regard cynicism as a personal defence mechanism whereby people prevent themselves to opening up to love and friendship for fear of being hurt. Others say it comes about due to a traumatic event that occurred in childhood and caused a person to "close up".

To be honest, it doesn't really matter what the "experts" say about the cause. The real task is to look inside yourself and find out why you are a cynic. Why do you think it came about? When did cynicism become a personal trait of yours? Why do you continue to think in a cynical way? You could study 1000 texts on cynicism for 1000 years but a single moment of genuine introspection will teach so much more. women are inclined to be discontented when they compare their positions to others and realise that they have less of what they believe themselves to be entitled than those around them. "Women in the highest place in position" is not a mission impossible, is conscious of your negative discrepancy between legitimate expectation and present actualities.

CHAPTER SIX
GROOMING TO LEAD

"It is the choices we are allowed to make that determine whether or not we break free or remained shackled." I had spent untold time spanning the world to survey the latest trend of interpretation given to the aforesaid assertion, until one early hours of the morning while I was caught up in a whirling vortex of emotion and the pounding of my own heart was the loudest noise in my apartment. The thought of redirection echoed in my head and I came to a conclusion that aged problems can be managed or probably solved by values and belief and that decision making principles and its strategically significant touch in the early stage of a child, connect his or her climbing faith. Hence I tried to make a research in quest of a real digital component to surmount these puzzles.

Her Excellency really touched on various issues including her career and the role of Nigerian women in training a girl child. She sees making of laws as a very sensitive procedure and it must be meticulously and painstakingly done both in politics and at home. The phrase "women liberation" to her is a thing of mind because she believes that human being are all liberated by the blood of Jesus; "God has not created any human being to be in bondage, "we have all been liberated." "It is obvious that in many cultures women are viewed and treated as inferior or as second-class citizens. Prejudices against them are deep-rooted. Gender-based violence in all its forms is an on-going problem, even in the so-called developed world. Relegating women to the background has been the order of the day. In the academic fields, some disciplines are classified as feminine in nature, thereby undermining the view of a girl child to see the opposite sex as a competitor. It is inconsistent with common sense to tell a girl that she fit professions like nurse, stewardess or something else that isn't at the top. But there's no reason she shouldn't be told that she should be the doctor, not the nurse, and if she wants to work on an airplane, she should fly the thing and don't serve drinks".

The fact that women have managed the intricacies and conflicts of raising a family, leave them well-qualified for arduous task and influential roles in the workforce. Judging from her indefatigable activities, Her Excellency brings to light the barrier of self-doubt that women frequently create, and shows why it is critical that women step up to the plate and fall into their natural roles as world leaders. So to clear these bugs and design flaws of the mind, it requires us to make an active choice among many plausible alternatives. Make choices that justify our past choices and then look for data to support them. And should steer clear of the most common wrong turns to be able to revamp a languishing society and be consistence in our stance, act with the complacency of the servant who values himself on his rank in servitude, and the imperturbability of the accurate calculator who has no illusion. Examine our needs rather than wants and true values rather than passing fads, because the inspiration and energy necessary to succeed in our lives, achieve harmony in personal relationship and reach inner peace, are all found in the gentle percolation of wisdom and inspiration endowed in a woman by God.

This manager bent to nurture next generation leaders emphasized on not training the girl child the right way, thereby spending over twenty years in building deeper skills in a narrow aspect. So to be able to use the right approach at the right time and change as the society demands is going to be necessary line of action in grooming to lead. "Yes women can sit on decision making table with the big men if they know how to command a presence, to have good judgment, and to make great decisions fast. You need to show strength and confidence and stand by your convictions."

She constantly emphasises on the need not to be swayed by naysayers or tough competition, most of all, to know how to motivate and inspire people to follow you. Most traits to life can be cultivated, boys are taught the hard way, to rough it up and clean up their tears and be the strongest child in their folk while girls are pampered so much without showing them how to tough it out in the world where the ceilings have more and more skylights. When you remind a girl child that she is capable of anything, she will not hesitate to challenge boys and set up a play dates with them. The task of being independent encourages her confidence to face challenges, so try and foster her independence in life and resist the urge of discouraging her while gathering momentum to fight when the tasks get much more intense. These are all in line with her teachings.

 Develop a culture of contempt for over pampering; find an activity that fosters teamwork for a girl child. Voluntary organizations can accord necessary assistance in encouraging leadership and collaboration and also nurture her competitively. Stories that highlight the activities of great women of substance and their adventures will go a long way to explicitly make the point that there are role models they can aspire to emulate. As a mother, a woman needs to act like a leader and be strong in convincing your child to follow your footstep instead of demanding it because she is a future leader and needs to break out of a click where she excels and aim for a bigger picture of the society. If they are better equipped intellectually, they can envisage a problem in a more informed way and counter it before it degenerates. That's a good methodology of ascending to power.

Grooming to lead can be challenging, teaching children problem solving for their future careers involve both direct and indirect role. Some Television programs can be so engrossing; slew of corruption and misbehaviour by lead characters can have negative influence, Shows flawed and interesting ways that real life can't support. These flawed characters somehow receive our sympathy and our encouragement. On the other hand, there are also numerous characters that display strength, intelligence, determination, tenacity, and passion that are both inspiring and motivating, so what program to watch should be properly guided. As you pursue a unique position to become a role model for the generation of women, try to play the role of a team player and a relationship builder. Women leaders foster commitment and creativity, serving as more of a teacher or coach rather than the more masculine. So the resolution you make that stick will give women even more ammunition to break down the long-protected image of men running the operations as women claw their way to the middle.

The stereotypes that plague women in the scene of competitions and workplace become nullified as the images you have created of a potential super power are being judiciously reconstructed to shape her day to day activities that will bring out strong leadership skills that rival those same skills in a man. The traits women have are a natural fit for a leadership model that promotes empathy and consensus building. Thereby conquering the conflicts between how fast you can move and how fast the society can move you because leadership is at its best when the vision is strategic, the voice persuasive and the results tangible.

Women need to capitalize on the educational advantage to sharpen their competitive edge and gain a positive step intrinsically for advancing in the workforce. So women will require more advanced degrees in different fields of endeavour, it will help in pursuing a strategy of increasing your contacts to include individuals that exercise power. Going out for lunch or drinks can be an extremely effective way to get to know people in your organization whom you rarely socialize with in the workplace or competitive environment. This can be a far more effective tactic than you might think. It just requires the willingness to step out of your immediate comfort zone. Formal or informal mentoring of younger women cannot be overemphasized because it will facilitate a good platform to groom younger women with leadership potential. "Nobody is going to step aside and just give us a seat at the table in the men dominated world. We have to make sure that we make a conscious effort to use all the tools at our disposal to make it happen." She affirmed. The tragedy of life is not that we die, but what dies inside a man while he lives" Albert Schweitzer.

CHAPTER SEVEN

SELF HELP

You're a woman, which means you're a work in progress. You are not amorphous; you are a vivacious flower waiting to be nipped. You are in the spotlight. You and God can do it together as long as you focus on what God can do and not on what you don't think you can do, what have you thought of doing? Dream remains mere dream if not actualized in essence. You are different from the other! It's you and only you and the power in you. We experience the fact of life that one human being is different in many ways from another, even in cases where two persons are identical twins. For this reason the Sages admonished: "Man, know thyself and after that be thyself; discover thine mission and strive to fulfil it for therein lies true happiness, the joy of living and success in life."

"Emancipate yourself from mental slavery" is decades' hackneyed aphorism, well scripted by Bob Marley in the lyrics of one of his numbers, titled 'redemption song'. The legend poetically admonished man to create his reality, create his future, and that destiny is what we make happened, not something that is imposed upon us. Furthermore, a bastion of freedom (LATE CHIEF GANI FAWEHINMI SAN) in his deep and abiding belief in the power of liberty, education, justice and equity, also admonished us that it is only when we turn our point of inquiry inward and attempt to realise our true self as a profound mystery of immense potential for good, that we come to the threshold of perceiving God.

If the Holy scriptures of the world, the Bhagavad Gita, the Vedas, the Upanishads, the Christian Bible, the Koran, etc., all concur about the temporary earthly status of man; if these great literatures are guides to true living , and we have increasing evidence that they are, we must ask ourselves certain salient questions. If indeed God created us in the image of God what more does a man need for God's sake in order to be a success in the business of living? Discover your niche in life and attain self-mastery through knowledge of self and your environment. We can see in this how man is a problem unto himself and therefore must be the one to sort it out in accordance with cosmic law. Take a moment to think if you are a remarkable woman; can you adapt to setbacks with optimism rather than self-doubt and pessimism? Can you set goals? Stick to deadlines, keep your word, be proactive, focus on the big picture, be your own cheerleader, sell yourself, etc. it gives you little mantras.

Every dream has a window called "hope" so you must understand that whoever advocate for progress and change will often pay a price. If you persevere, and see that you are fighting for changes that can happen, that will benefit you, your daughters and granddaughters, then you begin to forge ahead for your rightful place in some arduous task like political landscape not only as candidates who run for or hold office but a contributor, as a person who actively participate in the political process as men do. Apply your self-help thinking method and resist the mind-set that there is no place for women because of apathy, indifference, fear and insecurity. Break the siege of political enslavement and economic depravity first with your thought and forge unity of purpose not to turn the political sword against you by surrendering power to men. A Buddhist notion has it that all unhappiness in life stems from your addiction of what you EXPECT to happen and how things "should" be. Let go of that thought, and fight for freedom. Your level to take risk and explore more people and try to expand, make a mark for you.

The fact that you are a member of a family means that you can stand before challenges and initiate fresh moves for survival which includes more than taking action against oppressors of women. Fresh moves that will give right hearted woman a way of life, free of injustice, by means of a superior form of advice, advice that will allow all humans to lead satisfying, Joyful lives free of poverty. To prosper in this standard of living, you will not need a large inheritance of money, good connections, or business acumen. The question is how can we achieve these?

Her Excellency, as a woman of substance has successfully built a platform and self-help structure that is conducive to economic and human development. Her success so far has cleared social anomie and moral putrescence for women, so they supposed to begin to take precipitate steps bordering on the marginalization and relegation of women to the background as the case may be. So her life style is a ringing indictment of those who have subjected themselves to self-denials. Their excuses have been repudiated.

Developing a "theory mind" early in life acted as a compass that directed her adventurous   ship of life and gave her the power to develop mentally and overcame mind-blindness that is ravaging our youths lately.

Mind-blindness can be described as a cognitive disorder where an individual is unable to attribute mental states to the self and other. As a result of this disorder the individual is unaware of others' mental states. The individual is also not capable of attributing beliefs and desires to others. This ability to develop a mental awareness of what is in the mind of an individual is known as the Theory of Mind. This allows one to attribute our behaviour and actions to various mental states such as emotions and intentions. Mind-blindness is associated with autism and Asperger's syndrome (AS) patients who tend to show deficits in social insight. In addition to autism, AS, and schizophrenia, Mind-blindness research has recently been extended to other disorders such as dementia, bi-polar disorders, anti-social personality disorders as well as normal aging. Generally speaking, the "Mind-blindness" theory asserts that young people with these conditions are delayed in developing a theory mind, which normally allows growing people to put themselves into someone else's shoes, to imagine their thoughts and feelings.

So her self-help attitude introduced some points in life in which a woman should start chasing and at the same time fixing but not giving up. Because your assessment will make you to realize that you don't need some people and the drama they bring. And focus on creating your name because is the totality of your personality, your reputation and your destiny. Then you see yourself overlapping schisms that have been widely characterized as feminine in nature, (always wanting to be bought over at a very cheap rate by their male opponent). So women should take up their intellectual arms against self-abnegation. "You can fool people sometime but you can't fool all the people all the time, now you have seen the light, stand up for your right."

So rather than relining into docility and conceded leadership space and activism to the men, women should translate these advances into meaningful gains and encourage themselves into political participation because its concept either in the liberal or Marxian tradition, frowns at any attempt, whether wittingly or unwittingly, to exclude any segment of the society on the basis of sex, religion, or any other socio-economic variables. Women in their natural and God given nature are very significant citizens. The philosophy that guide human beings does not give women boldness for corruption, any woman that whiff of corruption trailed her exit from leadership position does not come back again because of shame. So women participation in competitive politics is a distinctive characteristic of democratic policies.

Huntington and Moore opined that substantial involvement of the citizenry in the political process, especially in elections, reflects and encourages a sense of democratic legitimacy that helps to contain violence and sustain the democratic policy. Powel, like many other liberal (Western) Scholar has equally emphasized this view, when he argues that without significant citizens' involvement in the political process, the democratic system falls short of its goals.

So the obvious conclusion is that women should put a stop to continued male-dominated and male-oriented misrule and say "enough is enough", "the time for positive change has arrived. The systematic entrenchment of practices aimed at the continued marginalisation of women in the political process must stop". So do not indulge in any discriminatory practices which will inhibit the girl-child, and tend to frustrate her socialization process as she grows up to see politics as the activity for men only.

While women participate fully in the life of the nation, yet, because of patriarchy, their participation is often ignored, undervalued, sometimes unrecorded or even obliterated. The contradiction is between participation on the one hand and social, political status and power on the other. Women's participation in politics is being frustrated by cultural inhibitions, lack of financial or economic power, domination by men, poor or total lack of education. So women should blend together, whether in or outside the corporate world, women must be responsible for their success, champions of their ideas and landscapers of their set goals. "Great careers are no longer passed down or handed over. They must be seeded, tended and grown—and you are the gardener. When women take their success into their own hands, when they take ownership of their achievements, development and ambition, there is no limit to what they can accomplish."

CHAPTER EIGHT
LEARN BY DOING

In Africa, the game of power is always played on a field too familiar to men since they were young, so they are always claiming to be comfortable on the platform and it's a game where winning remains constant and obvious on one part, and where aggression, self-promotion, and an effective display of power are the signs of a winner on the other. Women who ventured into the game, gallop disadvantaged, having been taught to be cooperative rather than competitive, to enjoy the process rather than simplify the terrain for them and to seek approval rather than assume success.

A woman of substance is a woman of power, a woman of positive influence and a woman of meaning. In her usual and encouraging ways of taking matters holistically, her Excellency sets out to level the playing arena by reeling out instructions on how men play and by teaching women to play smarter and win on their own terms. The challenges are still there. The men still look at women, oh, this is men's world. But there is nothing manly about it because what are required are your intellect and not your gender. In politics, for example, In the Legislature, there are no men; there are no women; what we have are Legislators.

You must engage yourself for you to learn. President Teddy Roosevelt spoke in his address titled "the man in the arena" where he said: "The credit belongs to the man who is actually in the arena, whose face is marred by dust and sweat and blood; who strives valiantly; who errs, who comes short again and again, because there is no effort without error and shortcoming; but who does actually strive to do the deeds; who knows great enthusiasms, the great devotions; who spends himself in a worthy cause; who at the best knows in the end the triumph of high achievement, and who at the worst, if he fails, at least fails while daring greatly, so that his place shall never be with those cold and timid souls who neither know victory nor defeat." you must strive to be counted as one.

She has these instructions, hoping that the best thing women can do for themselves is to think positively, expect positive things to happen, and do positive things and they will always get positive results. "Any time spent on negative thoughts is wasted time. Power, like the earth, is God's. He entrusts it to which he pleases. Not for its lure or to make a great show of it. With this knowledge therefore, I assume this onerous responsibility believing in the continuous support of people, relying on God for inner strength to remain firm in the right, for courage to give hope where there is hopeless, succour to the disadvantaged, and to give such a good account of my stewardship."

In Democracy for example, everything is all about the people. It must have human face in form of improved standard of living and general well-being of the people. Touching Lives should be the preoccupation of a woman of substance. The more you do it, the more you feel fulfilled, because of the enormity of economic woes facing people, hence the establishment of a platform the Growing Girls and Women in Nigeria Programme (GWIN); a gender-responsive budgeting system, and the highly acclaimed Youth Enterprise with Innovation Programme (YouWIN); to support entrepreneurs, that created thousands of jobs. This program has been evaluated by the World Bank as one of the most effective of its kind globally.

Women coming into politics should weigh their capability and capacity to cope. They should as well take into consideration, the constraints and limitations of their traditions and culture. Politics should not erode the traditional obligations of women. This will make the people to repel you instead of welcoming you. When you are at home, in your husband's house, you are a wife and a woman, a mother and a cook. But when you are in the corridors of power and career, you are a different personality.

Lots of people insinuate that women are unlikely to have a career and a good home. That is erroneous inference because a woman of substance combines a happy home and a rapidly progressing career. So this woman of excellence is compelling women to be a judge in their own case when they are faced with the conflict of reason whereby they must recognise the moral quality of a concrete act that they are going to perform, is in the process of performing, or has already completed. She also empowers them to reach an individual spiritual truth through reason and conscience. She further buttressed the definition of conscience as an aptitude, faculty, intuition or judgment of the intellect that distinguishes right from wrong.

"So the fact that we at times may have failed to act appropriately and decisively in one matter, shouldn't confine us to a perpetual paralysis of the will to do good in other matters. Fear of criticism, loss of political expediency should never deter us from our sacred duty. The conscience of the conscious mind is priceless. We must endure cravings until right conduct culminates in right mindfulness and right contemplation. Our conscience is our sword to flush mediocrity. It's all up to women! There are high hopes pinned on us because we can lend a hand for a positive change and modify the system into a people-friendly one." She said.

So, "nothing is terminal, everything is transitional. Every end is a new beginning. Don't let faces faze you. Phases are passages and passages are never dead ends, what looks like the end of the road will turn out to be a bend." Robert H. Schuler.

CHAPTER NINE
THE MAKING OF A WOMAN OF SUBSTANCE

Choosing to experience life outside of our comfort zone to gain good judgement that can be used in solving problems would appear to be an action that would lead to becoming a person of substance. People of substance know that there is no middle/neutral position on anything. They identify with the sentiment that "If you are not part of the solution, then you are part of the problem." Now just as wants outnumber means to satisfy them, so too, problems outnumber solutions and real problem solvers in life are few and far between. Good problem solving between competing interests typically requires a person of sound judgement who has immense empathy, complete objectivity and solid life-honed values.

Women of substance are made not born. According to Patrice O'Neal, it is a wide notion that average woman has typically little to offer of value to a man other than her body, in this opinion, some women characteristically show the world that they are even self-aware and monopolise the fact by narcissistically spending all their time beautifying themselves, accentuating the only real asset that they have in order to gain power by becoming dominant in the realm of superficiality.

However, he stressed that women of substance, have proved wrong the insinuation that everywoman is nothing other than a glorified excuse of a series of immoral holes, because such "dehumanisation" harms their ego, damaging the core of who they are, the outward persona that they've built up around themselves and the very narcissism they look to reinforce to feed this persona via external social validation; now cue a tirade of dopamine hits from filtered Instagram selfies, Facebook likes and her inability to put down a smart phone combined with a rigorous routine of careful makeup application and carefully selected clothing choices.

A woman of substance is a woman of power, class, a positive influence, a woman of meaning and all that is good and bold. To be branded a woman of substance is one of the greatest compliments and achievement one can give to a woman that want to be an influential female. So these add to qualities that make this great woman of substance.

1. To be happy the way she is. It is such a relief to realize that being different and imperfect is far more interesting than being a perfect person .Accepting the way you are and feel happy as yourself just the way you are, signifies the word beauty. A woman of substance doesn't let the high demands and expectations get them down; especially with pressure put on women in today's society so immense. A woman should not let the likes of perfected image or criticism affect her, be happy and appreciate the way you are.

2. Speak out her opinions. A woman of substance never fails when it comes to voicing her opinions or standing up on what she believes in. She says what she thinks, what's she believes in and argue what she don't. She knows when to speak and the time to keep quite. She never keeps quiet when her voice is undermined and she fights for poor and weak and among the strong voices her voice is heard and people around her never get disappointed by the power of her voice and her wish becomes their command.

3. She knows what she wants and pursues it. A woman of substance knows from the beginning what she wants and works towards achieving it. She always

follows her heart and she never gives up. Other people's opinion comes as a proposal for her to oppose or accept but not get swayed and follow the majority. She press on even when she feels there is no more hope. She is a go getter. She remains a lion in the park and refuses to surrender to grass even when economy is not conducive.

4. Live up to her morals and values. A woman of substance is a person of moral and values in life. Her morals and values inspire her, motivate and strengthen her will to do something significant in the world. She never changes her morals to impress anyone but instead she stands with her moral and values which makes her natural and a treasure to many. She lives by her morals and values in life and she is aware of them. Being a woman of substance requires effort and application. She never quit instead she always aim to perspire, aspire and transpire!!

Heed me when I say that all women of substance are trained by men, they are not magically born out of the womb, and a "unicorn" is merely a high quality woman of substance raised, cultivated and overseen by men of value, integrity and intelligence. Whether that man is her father or later on, a serious boyfriend, she is trained and maintained by men to be a quality woman. To an extent she is trained by her mother also, who respects the strength of an authoritarian man and imparts the ideas of the father onto her daughter by proxy, but a mother who was unable to secure a strong man, in her bitterness and ineptitude, will typically not pass on conducive moral and sexual values that will lead to romantic success for her daughter. After all, she cannot do for her daughter what she was unable to obtain for herself.

Often a woman who is of quality from a young age, non-promiscuous, good-natured, talented, intelligent, humorous, not hateful of men and emotionally stable is a woman who has had a good relationship with her father. Her father having been what for lack of a better term is considered an alpha male, instilling positive traits into her psyche with a firm, loving hand, raising her to respect men and accommodate them in the social contract; rather than hold them in contempt and challenge them as adversaries like mainstream society would indoctrinate.

It is the job of the man who commits to such a woman romantically to then maintain the legacy that her father left, good girls will turn bad in the absence of a strong male figure, for it is woman's emotional transient nature which causes them to stray from the path of romantic success. It is woman's emotional nature whether she consciously desires it or not that necessitates her need for strong trustworthy leadership, so that she may absolve herself of responsibility in her inevitable moments of weakness, she wants someone to lean on but fears that the dissolution of that responsibility will be abused, a connection of trust to a powerful man is what women crave.

In essence, this is why women tend to look for "men who were like their fathers" they seek dominance in which they can trust, and it is this dominance which allows them to remain emotionally stable, offloading their neuroticism onto the stoicism of the man that they pair with. Good women are not only made by men, but must also be maintained by men. In the absence of such leadership, women take on detrimental qualities in the name of "freedom", being poor leaders themselves (due to the erraticism of emotionalism) and in the absence of authority (typically a strong patriarch and an equally traditional matriarch) they become feral and pursue self-destruction, always chasing the nearest perceivable "emotional high", rather than planning ahead for the days where the temporary adrenaline-filled joyful experience that short-term liaisons provide are no longer available to them as their sexual appeal evaporates with age, leaving them without legacy and family with a firm foot in spinsterhood.

Essentially, all women have daddy issues (no I'm not going to qualify that as "most" or "some" but forthrightly tell you **ALL**), if he was a good father she wants a serious relationship with a man who was like her father, strong, compassionate, worldly, a badass, but with a soft spot unique to her, women love to feel special, in fact, they crave it. If she had a good father, as a man looking to date such a woman (a woman with a good father) your life has already been made infinitely easier by his diligence, he has already raised an appealing woman and then left the foundations in place to cultivate this valuable raw material into a long-term partner, a mother and a wife. However, the onus is on you to be strong enough to maintain the status quo, such a woman will not respect weakness and thus will not follow the lead of a man who is too inept to take charge, such a woman will hold you to the standard set by her father and as such will compare you both in starkness.

If her father was absent or otherwise a let-down, she wants her man to be everything he wasn't, her mind has filled in the blanks with what he should have been, some of that of course will be complete fantastical nonsense. What she will want in this scenario is for a man to essentially fill the emotional void the lack of a father figure left her with, whilst perversely in simultaneity she will find it hard to trust men due to her sense of abandonment. Maintaining a healthy, loving and conducive relationship with such a woman will be exceptionally difficult. She will effectively be both her own as well as your own worst enemy, actively sabotaging everything you're trying to build with all the irrationality of her delinquency manifesting itself in the present day as morbid insecurity.

This is why women with poor relationships with their fathers are a massive red flag. When eying up a woman for a prospective long-term romantic engagement, find out what her relationship with her father is like, the absence of a father or a negative relationship with her father are massive red flags as she is already set-up to be a poor romantic prospect, mainly due to how she was (or wasn't) raised. Single mothers quite simply are inept to raise quality children singlehandedly. The presence of a weak father is better than nothing, but typically you want her to have had a father who was a patriarch, a dominant man who taught her discipline so that her base schematic of "what men should be like" is healthy and isn't formed from unhealthy feminist stereotypes and the ramblings of a bitter and romantically unsuccessful single mother. Still, even the presence of a patriarch in a young girl's life isn't always enough to ensure a quality woman; as the prevailing socially engineered cultural forces around her proactively do their utmost to undermine the will and intent that her father's best interests have for her.

Red pill women are not "unicorns", they are women capable of curbing their instincts whilst using logic to be more desirable in an effort to secure provisioning in their old age, effectively they're investing in the long-game and have been made self-aware enough to realise that being a slut getting by on her sexuality and youth is not a gravy train that is going to last forever. They are women who will compromise and work with a man who is equally strong enough and patient enough to deal with them. Everything is a compromise with women, whether she's a cunt, has BPD, is unintelligent or is as high-calibre and well cultivated as an emotionally stable and feminine red pill woman, the inherent difference between masculine and feminine nature leads to a process of unending compromise.

No matter the woman, she will test your patience; this is just women full-stop. Not got a lot of patience? Women are going to just piss you the hell off then. It does help however when a woman can offset this inherently annoying trait of trying a man's patience by bringing more than merely a sex to the table. As a man you should be informed that an inherently irrational being is going to do nothing but antagonise the patience of someone who thinks in logic rather than the cognitive cartwheels of reactive transient emotionalism.

The biggest flattery of all to women, which only an intelligent woman will realise, is that despite the sheer frustration and pain she causes him with her volatile emotivity, is that such a man still chooses to stick with her and provide for her despite her shortcomings. A female's self-awareness of his sacrifice and a declaration of appreciation for that sacrifice go a long way to help reconcile the huge fundamental differences in expectation that men and women have of each other, women being far more audaciously demanding and stringently needy by nature of their disposition than men are.

It is somewhat insane how the appreciation of an intrinsically irrational woman within the paradigm of a relationship is valued so intimately by the romantic disposition of what is otherwise a rational man. It is often true after all that we value that which is hardest to obtain, and a woman's appreciation is scarcely given in earnest.

CHAPTERTEN

KEYS TO LEADERSHIP

"If you have a sense of purpose that drives you, then aim high and become a leader and make room as you go" Dr. Ngozi Okonjo-Iweala.

Most people don't realize that leadership is fundamentally about service, about a dying to self and loving others into their true potential. It isn't about us personally. It isn't about what we can get, or consume. It isn't about elevating ourselves above others. It isn't about ego. Leadership is about lowering ourselves such that the people who work with us, and our organizations can thrive in ways that create value (economic and social)."

"When I am serving I can't help but to be compassionate. And when I am not, the tendency to become jaded, more callous, and less forgiving can take over. This has been one of my greatest observations since leaving my law practice. How ineffective business leaders are once they lose the capacity to put themselves to the side in favour of the common good." Binta Niambi Brown.

"Leadership is mostly about listening. You can't create a team that thrives if you can't respond to what each member needs. They don't always ask directly. And outwardly, you can't break through the chatter in the marketplace if you can't hear and respond directly to what the audience is asking for."

Collins says that through observing leaders and being managed herself, she's discovered that the best teams to work on were the ones with the best communicators–not just in term of articulating a vision, but also to respond to individual personalities on a team in effective ways. *Jessanne Collins.*

"I think to be a good leader; you really need to learn humility. To give credit to your subordinates when things go well, and to shoulder the responsibility when things hit the fan. It's hard, but I think the lack of ego is something that people respect and appreciate."

Moreland tells *Fast Company* she learned this lesson when starting her company because no matter how much you want to deflect responsibility or assign blame when things go bad, ultimately, those at the top are responsible. ***Brooke Moreland.***

"Most acts of leadership happen behind closed doors. In that sense, a leader's journey is actually quite private. It has to be; the conversations with an employee; the hard decisions at a board meeting; and the thoughts in bed late at night. It's counter-intuitive because we think of leaders as very public figures."

"I think one of the biggest ways that I learned this lesson has been through personal relationships with other leaders. Specifically the relationships that have moved beyond business and into true friendship where there's a certain level of trust and camaraderie,"

"I remember one time in particular, I had just started to become friends with the leader of a popular start-up. I was kind of in awe of this particular CEO and had just read a particular article about some of her glorious achievements. I remember talking to her soon after the article came out and she was talking about the people that she needed to lay off and some of the office drama. I saw a whole new side of her leadership based on how she handled those private matters. And I realized that those things that take up so much time and energy and emotion–and that really define us as leaders–are usually private situations." ***Jody Porowski.***

"Leadership is asking a lot of questions. I've learned that between customers, employees and all our stakeholders, my number one job is asking [my team] a lot of questions so I can serve them. They are on the front lines dealing with customers or wearing our products and while I am steering the ship, they are the engine and the propellers. I have to be responsive to what they need and often people are too busy or bogged down to even articulate what they need." ***Monif Clark.***

"Don't be afraid to be you and own it. If you think being a leader is about having some agenda, it's not. Being a leader is actually being completely with who you are and speaking from that place, giving feedback, sharing opinions from that place. That's why people follow you."

Ringelmann tells *Fast Company* she learned this lesson when changing roles at Indiegogo and realised that power is all about the ability to truly influence people and make an impact in their lives. "It doesn't come from any title or position … a true leader is someone who is wholeheartedly willing to be their authentic self." ***Danae Ringelman.***

"There's a lot of talk about being a born leader … having natural leadership. I think that's a myth. My experience is that if you are not paying attention to the things you're doing wrong, then you're not evolving and learning. I would say that leadership is something that is learned. It can be learned and should be learned. Leadership is something you're always honing and learning and reflecting to see ways you could have been better at it. Anyone who thinks they're a natural leader is probably horrible to work with." ***Rachel Sklar.***

"Sometimes you just have to make a leap of faith. As I was moving up the ranks, sometimes I'd be in a meeting and think, 'we really need a decision here,' and realise a beat later it was me who had to make that decision. Leadership is about presenting confidence and decisiveness. Of course it's best if this is how you're really feeling at the moment but it's possible–in fact necessary–to make decisions you're not 100 percent sure of. The longer you do it the more natural going with your gut becomes. And then soon you start giving advice like 'just go with your gut.'" ***Anne Fulenwider.***

"When it's a smaller team, you can rapidly make changes because you're all sitting in the same room together, looking at each other," she tells *Fast Company*. "As teams get bigger, I have to be very careful about the advice I give. If the founders ask me, I tell them my opinion, but as teams get bigger, the more I really have to listen."

In a leadership position, Rae says you need to train yourself on "deep listening" so that you can really understand what's going on. "You lead with much more true confidence when you understand how people around you–whether they agree or disagree with your decision–will react. In that way, you'll be able to pull them along with you even if they don't agree with you … by the way, this works in marriage too." ***Katie Rae.***

Her Excellency, Dr. Ngozi Okonjo-iweala, having brought to light the barrier of self-doubt that women frequently create, and showed why it is critical that women step up to the plate and fall into their natural roles as world leaders and also cleared these bugs and design flaws of the mind, whilst continuing showing the way to make an active choice among many plausible alternatives. Coming in terms with the above assertions and more, together with proofs that leaders are not some sort of 'all-knowing-beings,' but trusting their instincts to lead them to an answer, has lived up to the sterling qualities of the author's concept in coining the title of this book. She is therefore the brain 'behind a woman of substance' and a character to be emulated as uncensored solution to women puzzles.

RELEVANT PROVERBS

Wisdom is wealth! One thing I respect deeply about Africa is the treasure of wisdom our ancestors have handed down to us. While some of our leaders may have forgotten them, the rest of us don't need to. From prudent sayings on wisdom itself, to judicious encouragements, warnings and even quirky advice on learning, patience, unity, wealth, poverty, community, family, love and marriage, these quotes will inspire you to be the best you can possibly be.

Those whose palm-kernels were cracked for them by a benevolent spirit should not forget to be humble.

- Wisdom is wealth. ~ Swahili
- Wisdom is like a baobab tree; no one individual can embrace it. ~ Akan proverb
- The fool speaks, the wise man listens. ~ Ethiopian proverb
- Wisdom does not come overnight. ~ Somali proverb
- The heart of the wise man lies quiet like limpid water. ~ Cameroon proverb
- Wisdom is like fire. People take it from others. ~ Hema (DRC) proverb
- Only a wise person can solve a difficult problem. ~ Akan proverb
- Knowledge without wisdom is like water in the sand. ~ Guinean proverb
- In the moment of crisis, the wise build bridges and the foolish build dams. ~ Nigerian proverb
- If you are filled with pride, then you will have no room for wisdom. ~ African proverb
- A wise person will always find a way. ~ Tanzanian proverb
- Nobody is born wise. ~ African proverb
- A man who uses force is afraid of reasoning. ~Kenyan proverb
- Wisdom is not like money to be tied up and hidden. ~ Akan proverb
- Learning expands great souls. ~ Namibian proverb
- To get lost is to learn the way. ~ African proverb
- By crawling a child learns to stand. ~ African proverb
- If you close your eyes to facts, you will learn through accidents. ~African proverb
- He, who learns, teaches. ~ Ethiopian proverb
- Wealth, if you use it, comes to an end; learning, if you use it, increases. ~ Swahili proverb
- By trying often, the monkey learns to jump from the tree. ~ Buganda proverb

- You always learn a lot more when you lose than when you win. ~ African proverb
- You learn how to cut down trees by cutting them down. ~ Betake proverb
- The wise create proverb for fools to learn, not to repeat. ~African proverb
- What you help a child to love can be more important than what you help him to learn. -African proverb
- By the time the fool has learned the game, the players have dispersed. ~Ashanti proverb
- One who causes others misfortune also teaches them wisdom. ~African proverb
- You do not teach the paths of the forest to an old gorilla. ~Congolese proverb
- What you learn is what you die with. ~African proverb
- Instruction in youth is like engraving in stone. ~Moroccan Proverb
- When you follow in the path of your father, you learn to walk like him. ~Ashanti Proverb
- Ears that do not listen to advice, accompany the head when it is chopped off. ~ African proverb
- Advice is a stranger; if he's welcome he stays for the night; if not, he leaves the same day. ~Malagasy Proverb
- Traveling is learning. ~Kenyan Proverb
- Where there are experts there will be no lack of learners. ~Swahili Proverb

Peace is costly but it is worth the expense. ~Kenyan proverb
War has no eyes ~ Swahili saying
When a king has good counselors, his reign is peaceful. ~Ashanti proverb
Peace does not make a good ruler. ~Botswana proverb
A fight between grasshoppers is a joy to the crow. ~ Lesotho proverb
There can be no peace without understanding. -Senegalese proverb
Milk and honey have different colors, but they share the same house peacefully. ~   African proverb

If you can't resolve your problems in peace, you can't solve war. ~ Somalian proverb
When there is peace in the country, the chief does not carry a shield. ~Ugandan proverb
When two elephants fight, it is the grass that gets trampled. ~ Swahili saying
Speak softly and carry a big stick; you will go far. ~ West African proverb

He who thinks he is leading and has no one following him is only taking a walk.
~ Malawian proverb
An army of sheep led by a lion can defeat an army of lions led by a sheep. ~
Ghanaian proverb
He who is destined for power does not have to fight for it. ~ Ugandan proverb
Do not forget what is to be a sailor because of being a captain yourself. ~
Tanzanian proverb
Without a leader, black ants are confused. ~Ugandan proverb
He who refuses to obey cannot command. ~ Kenyan proverb
He who fears the sun will not become chief. ~Ugandan proverb
A large chair does not make a king. ~ Sudanese proverb
Because he lost his reputation, he lost a kingdom. ~ Ethiopian proverb
Where a woman rules, streams run uphill. ~ Ethiopian proverb
A leader who does not take advice is not a leader. ~ Kenyan proverb
If the cockroach wants to rule over the chicken, then it must hire the fox as a
body-guard. ~ Sierra Leone proverb

Unity is strength, division is weakness. ~ Swahili proverb

Sticks in a bundle are unbreakable. ~ Bondei proverb

It takes a village to raise a child. ~African proverb
Cross the river in a crowd and the crocodile won't eat you. ~African proverb
Many hands make light work. ~ Haya (Tanzania) proverb
Where there are many, nothing goes wrong. ~ Swahili proverb
Two ants do not fail to pull one grasshopper. ~ Tanzanian proverb
A single bracelet does not jingle. ~ Congolese proverb
A single stick may smoke, but it will not burn. ~African proverb
If you want to go quickly, go alone, If you want to go far, go together. ~ African
proverb

- A family is like a forest, when you are outside it is dense, when you are
  inside you see that each tree has its place. ~ African Proverb
- A united family eats from the same plate. ~ Buganda proverb
- A family tie is like a tree, it can bend but it cannot break. ~ African
  proverb
- If I am in harmony with my family, that is success. ~ Ute proverb
- Brothers love each other when they are equally rich. ~ African proverb
- Dine with a stranger but save your love for your family. ~ Ethiopian
  proverb
- There is no fool who is disowned by his family. ~ African proverb
- Home affairs are not talked about on the public square. ~ African
  proverb
- If relatives help each other, what evil can hurt them? ~ African proverb

- He who earns calamity, eats it with his family. ~ African proverb
- Dine with a stranger but save your love for your family. ~ Ethiopian proverb
- The old woman looks after the child to grow its teeth and the young one in turn looks after the old woman when she loses her teeth. ~ Akan (Ghana, Ivory Coast) proverb
- When brothers fight to the death, a stranger inherits their father's estate. ~ Ibo proverb
- Children are the reward of life. ~ African proverb
- To be without a friend is to be poor indeed. ~ Tanzanian proverb
- Hold a true friend with both hands. ~ African proverb
- The friends of our friends are our friends. ~ Congolese proverb
- A friend is someone you share the path with. ~ African proverb
- Show me your friend and I will show you your character. ~ African proverb
- Return to old watering holes for more than water; friends and dreams are there to meet you. ~ African proverb
- Between true friends even water drunk together is sweet enough. ~ African proverb
- A small house will hold a hundred friends. ~ African proverb
- A close friend can become a close enemy.~ African proverb
- Bad friends will prevent you from having good friends. ~ Gabon proverb
- Make some money but don't let money make you. ~ Tanzania
- It is no shame at all to work for money. ~ Africa
- He who loves money must labor. ~ Mauritania
- By labor comes wealth. ~ Yoruba
- Poverty is slavery. ~Somalia
- One cannot both feast and become rich. ~ Ashanti
- One cannot count on riches. ~ Somalia
- Money is sharper than the sword. – Ashanti
- A man's wealth may be superior to him. ~ Cameroon
- The rich are always complaining. ~ Zulu
- The wealth which enslaves the owner isn't wealth. ~ Yoruba
- The poor man and the rich man do not play together. ~ Ashanti
- Lack of money is lack of friends; if you have money at your disposal, every dog and goat will claim to be related to you. ~ Yoruba
- With wealth one wins a woman. ~ Uganda
- Dogs do not actually prefer bones to meat; it is just that no one ever gives them meat. ~ Akan
- A real family eats the same cornmeal. ~ Bayombe
- If your cornfield is far from your house, the birds will eat your corn. ~ Congo
- Money can't talk, yet it can make lies look true. ~ South Africa

- One cannot count on riches. ~ Somalia
- Money is not the medicine against death. ~ Ghana
- He who receives a gift does not measure. ~ Africa
- Much wealth brings many enemies. – Swahili
- There is no one who became rich because he broke a holiday; no one became fat because he broke a fast. ~ Ethiopia
- What you give you get, ten times over. ~ Yoruba
- Greed loses what it has gained. ~ Africa
- You become wise when you begin to run out of money. ~ Ghana
- If ten cents does not go out, it does not bring in one thousand dollars. ~ Ghana
- You should not hoard your money and die of hunger. – Ghana
- Wealth diminishes with usage; learning increases with use. ~ Nigeria
- Wisdom is not like money to be tied up and hidden. ~ Akan
- Having a good discussion is like having riches ~ Kenya
- Knowledge is better than riches. ~ Cameroon
- You must act as if it is impossible to fail. ~ Ashanti
- Do not let what you cannot do tear from your hands what you can. ~ Ashanti
- One who plants grapes by the road side, and one who marries a pretty woman, share the same problem. ~Ethiopian Proverb
- Beautiful from behind, ugly in front. ~Uganda Proverb
- The skin of the leopard is beautiful, but not his heart. ~Baluba proverb
- Ugliness with a good character is better than beauty. ~Nigerian Proverb
- A beautiful one hurts the heart. African Proverb
- Anyone who sees beauty and does not look at it will soon be poor. ~Yoruba Proverb
- The surface of the water is beautiful, but it is no good to sleep on. ~Ghanaian Proverb
- If there is character, ugliness becomes beauty; if there is none, beauty becomes ugliness. ~Nigerian Proverb
- You are beautiful, but learn to work, for you cannot eat your beauty. ~Congolese Proverb
- The one who loves an unsightly person is the one who makes him beautiful. ~Ganda Proverb
- Having beauty doesn't mean understanding the perseverance of marriage. ~ African Proverb
- You are beautiful because of your possessions. ~Baguirmi Proverb
- Every woman is beautiful until she speaks. ~Zimbabwean Proverb
- Three things cause sorrow to flee; water, green trees, and a beautiful face. ~Moroccan Proverb
- A beautiful thing is never perfect. ~Egyptian Proverb
- Patience is the mother of a beautiful child. ~Bantu Proverb
- There is no beauty but the beauty of action. ~Moroccan Proverb

- Judge not your beauty by the number of people who look at you, but rather by the number of people who smile at you. ~ African Proverb
- A pretty face and fine clothes do not make character. ~Congolese Proverb
- Youth is beauty, even in cattle. ~Egyptian Proverb
- A pretty basket does not prevent worries. ~Congolese Proverb
- It's those ugly caterpillars that turn into beautiful butterflies after seasons. ~ African Proverb
- The most beautiful fig may contain a worm. ~Zulu Proverb
- It is only a stupid cow that rejoices at the prospect of being taken to a beautiful abattoir. ~ African Proverb
- A woman who pursues a man for sex loses her spiritual beauty. ~ African Proverb
- A chicken with beautiful plumage does not sit in a corner. ~ African Proverb
- The cook does not have to be a beautiful woman. ~Shona Proverb
- Beautiful words don't put porridge in the pot. ~Botswana Proverb
- She is beautiful; she has love, understands; she respects herself and others; everyone likes, loves and honors her; she is a goddess. ~ African Proverb
- There is always a winner even in a monkey's beauty contest. ~ African Proverb
- Dress up a stick and it'll be a beautiful bride. ~Egyptian Proverb
- An ugly child of your own is more to you than a beautiful one belonging to your neighbor. ~Ganda Proverb
- Even the colors of a chameleon are for survival not beauty. ~ African Proverb
- Beautiful discourse is rarer than emerald ~ yet it can be found among the servant girls at the grindstones. ~Egyptian Proverb
- When a once-beautiful piece of cloth has turned into rags, no one remembers that it was woven by Ukwa master weavers. ~Igbo Proverb
- A woman's polite devotion is her greatest beauty. ~ African Proverb
- There are many colorful flowers on the path of life, but the prettiest have the sharpest thorns. ~ African Proverb
- He who marries a beauty marries trouble. ~Nigerian Proverb
- Despite the beauty of the moon, sun and the stars, the sky also has a threatening thunder and striking lightening. ~ African Proverb
- Getting only a beautiful woman is like planting a vine on the roadside everyone feeds on it. ~ African Proverb
- Greatness and beauty do not belong to the gods alone. ~Nigerian Proverb
- Roosters' tail feathers: pretty but always behind. ~Malagasy Proverb
- Beauty is not sold and eaten. ~Nigerian Proverb
- She is like a road – pretty, but crooked. ~Cameroonian Proverb

- Why they like an ugly person takes long for a beautiful person to know. ~ African Proverb
- If you find "Miss This Year" beautiful, then you'll find "Miss Next Year" even more so. ~Nigerian Proverb
- The beauty of a woman becomes useless if there is no one to admire it. ~ African Proverb
- He who loves the vase loves also what is inside. ~ African proverb
- It's much easier to fall in love than to stay in love. ~ African proverb
- Coffee and love taste best when hot. ~ Ethiopian proverb
- Where there is love there is no darkness. ~Burundian proverb
- If you are ugly you must either learn to dance or make love. ~ Zimbabwean Proverb
- Pretend you are dead and you will see who really loves you. ~ African proverb
- To love the king is not bad, but a king who loves you is better. ~ Wolof proverb
- A happy man marries the girl he loves, but a happier man loves the girl he marries. ~ African proverb
- If you marry a monkey for his wealth, the money goes and the monkey remains as is. ~ Egyptian proverb
- Love never gets lost it's only kept. ~ African proverb
- Never marry a woman who has bigger feet than you. ~ Mozambique proverb
- One thread for the needle, one love for the heart. ~ Sudanese proverb
- Love has to be shown by deeds not words. ~ Swahili proverb
- Love is a despot who spares no one. ~Namibian proverb
- Marriage is like a groundnut; you have to crack it to see what is inside. ~ Ghanaian proverb
- Patience is the key which solves all problems. ~ Sudanese proverb
- Hurry, hurry has no blessings. ~ Swahili proverb
- Patience is the mother of a beautiful child. ~ Bantu proverb
- To run is not necessarily to arrive. ~ Swahili proverb
- Patience can cook a stone. ~ African proverb
- A patient man will eat ripe fruit. ~ African proverb
- At the bottom of patience one finds heaven. ~ African proverb
- A patient person never misses a thing. ~ Swahili proverb
- Patience puts a crown on the head. ~ Ugandan proverb
- Patience attracts happiness; it brings near that which is far. ~ Swahili proverb
- Always being in a hurry does not prevent death; neither does going slowly prevent living. ~ Ibo proverb
- However long the night, the dawn will break. ~ African proverb (personal favourite!)

www.ingramcontent.com/pod-product-compliance
Lightning Source LLC
Chambersburg PA
CBHW070229260726
48658CB00006BA/2243